an/other pastoral

by
Tjawangwa Dema

with illustrations by Tebogo Cranwell

and a foreword by Chris Abani

NO BINDINGS

nobindings.co.uk

Published by No Bindings Ltd, 2022

Printed in England by Earthbound Press

ISBN 978-1-9997372-2-1

The cover is printed on recycled paper.
The pages are printed on FSC certified paper.

Contents

Foreword

Intensity and anticipation: these two feelings describe the visceral effect of entering Tjawangwa Dema's new collection. In short, dense lyrics of compressed, emotional fervour, Tjawangwa Dema journeys through a world made external from deep but deft meditations on self, identity, race, politics, loss, recuperation and a certain three-dimensional cartography that relies on negative space and texture, like a handprint in ochre on a rough African desert rock.

The body here precedes all things in the world; before thought, before language, is this body, at once real but sculpted. All the memory, lineages and all that has preceded us, yet flows new from us. An amalgamation of all the earths that have come before us. This is the evocation in these poems, and urgent too, as though to say, when we say environment, we mean only as my body finds its way, when we say climate, we mean as I feel it on this largest of organs, skin. When we say cartography, we mean to chart, to map, not the world but this body's journey through the world and this means, the world as I know and see and think. The compass that guides us in these engaged poems, that burn with a quiet ferocity, is the hope of a body upright, 90 degrees to the earth, self and shadow, body and world.

The images by Tebogo Cranwell are a perfect complement for a poetic vehicle because not only do they become poems of a kind themselves, with the brilliant use of spring-loaded lines and negative space, but also because in this way, the narrative surrenders to the lyric, creating an intimacy that results from a form inviting connection and allowing us to bring all of ourselves into this space. But to be clear, space here does not mean empty, but rather, possibility, potential. There is a polyvocality, a vast chorus of voices and ideas and even ancestors present here that root firmly in the tradition of African orality and oratory but now in the written form, they last longer, allowing a multitude of psychological archetypes, of the old and new, to renegotiate the terms of self and being. The true power of the mythic.

In both poetic image and drawn image, the definite shape becomes like water, holding everything that is brought to it. The body appearing as a mark on the world canvas. A mark that stands in sharp angled relationship to the earth. A mark wavering in the shimmer of a hot African plane. A simple sketch that fills in the world. In these poems, Tjawangwa Dema, with deft moves, turns lyric and narrative lines into a fierce, political and artistic engagement that reverses the erasure of living black bodies, living black culture. A vast reclamation of the world.

And so, we have a vital hymnal to blackness, not as response, or reaction, or even address. This is a powerful anthem to self; this self happens to be black with all the power and threat of that.

Chris Abani
Chicago, 2022

For the leadwood trees of Mmadikola.
Ya matswere a Mmadikola.

Prologue: Hypothesis

where bank slips its mouth open
to let a river happen,
you say *go.*
the word is the cruellest flower –
english broom, white snakeroot,
an angel's trumpet, so i stay.
sure as cocksfoot,
as at home as the wind, elsewhere, everywhere
i insist on the same, slow walk
unfurl a picnic of apples –
braeburn – carried in each pocket.
glad they survived, no car, i took a train
and two buses i could little afford to get here.
still your lips, so tight they are foxglove
on the translucence of your face,
your english too sheathed
to speak and mean at the same time.

and when it rains i miss desert,
miss sun, miss baobab,
i mean home,
my grandfather, not unlike yours,
on a field somewhere
though fields and fields apart,
so far apart an ocean nestles there.
and now we are not quite here
together, you and i

until a child dismantles distance
in her bright bee'd plastic boots,
her small arms nettling
the wobble-dance of grass

she's saying *hello*
and more
with her small, curious face.
i've found the blackberries.
she wants to know *how?*

i am made brave – despite your face
say to her, *where I'm from,*
the honeyguide bird tells you
where the honey is. she cannot herself
breach the hive and so she calls and
calls for you to help.
all nature speaks if we listen
oak, pine, bracken, sheep, eel,
human

i've kept my distance,
knelt farther than i would with my own child.
a talking bird? she says.
you reach out, dam her flow
but the river of her giggle runs through us,
its old syntax not quite undoing of veldt
nor airport or boat
nor this open field.
more an unexpected door,
the opening to a big top –
a circus cock-eyed in the head.
i imagine an elephant,
trampling your old thoughts
and sense your mind ungive quietly
perhaps, perhaps surprised
that i in my chain-store waterproofs
might know a thing.

here is the line between man and man
                                              and nature,
man-made
                                              as all false boundaries are.

why
is there under that poem always
an other poem?
—Lucille Clifton, 'surely i am able to write poems'

The best way to access these different skeletons was to produce
a form, not a spineless one but a tense and energy-charged one.
In any case, this text is one on whose surface the reader can glide
freely, without control points or visas, sojourning as long as desired,
moving about at will, returning and leaving at any moment and
through any door.
—Achille Mbembe, *Necropolitics*

Prosthesis

& since i cannot swim
i span myself into a fathom
lay my body down as a plea
upon the water
let my four-year-old self
drown again

i do this
as an offering
my grey hair resisting the water's slick fingers
is buoyant
a half float returning to its true shape
while i contort myself
all fear & no grace
each stroke
a beating
on that which cannot scar

the instructor says *feel the water*
mouth closed
i want to say i feel all of it
pull & push
drift & dunk
its wet yank & toss
now & in all its befores

more camel than crocodile
between gulps i glance back at my son
on the shore
learning what water isn't
for him i lean into the wake of its open palm

may he never know
that a crossing does not mean better
            safer

that what the shield depicts as walking
on water
is how i stay drowning
an island for his small body to rest upon
i make a bridge of blood & bone
of sinew & lung
for him
i swallow salt
take one last breath
above the shimmer
drown again
& again

Innocence

This Is Not a Matter For

July third twenty twenty-one
last night we set the ocean on fire
this is not a metaphor
the Gulf of Mexico is on fire
I want to say what really happened was
but ears pinned back we jar and stomp
think the whole thing a divot
yet what's done cannot be undone
though we pour water on water

Neema and Mpho want a sleepover / So much happens overnight
that I'm scared to let my daughter go / *We're in the middle
of a pandemic* we say / So young / Every time they turn
their heads / They think what's behind them
has disappeared

August twenty-twenty
the Amazon is on fire
we've never *seen* so much fire
we are rich with flames and smoke and ash
miles and miles of devastation
from outer space it looks like
the shape of not listening
the texture of not giving a fuck
what comes next
when the green men come
and they are not green or men
supplicant to having like us
which pyromaniac shall we take them to
this is not a matter for the bankers
or the billionaires in their shuttles
forget the moon and Mars

we've finally done it
altered our object
its permanence
we are enchanted by loss
this is what our having brings us

Our refusal behind them / Neema and Mpho still want a sleepover /
So much happens overnight that I'm scared to let my daughter go /
We give them colouring pens instead / Tell them to draw each other
through computer screens / Tell them what we always tell them / Now /
We're in the middle of a pandemic / So young they don't know
we mean / Every time / Real time / All time now / That *we* set it up
so it'll always be a pandemic / Virus or fire / Colour or body /
Plenty of nothing

Black Bear in the Grocery Store

here we are in Thousand Oaks –
cypress trees in the grue distance –
milk in one hand and the other out-
stretched
fetching
when we are stupefied in the land of plenty
of aisles and aisles of having
what is canned   bottled   preserved   fresh
all must be paid for
in this tiled valley of dead things
between steel streams full with multi-coloured plastic
and paper packages and tin flowers
and below the m&ms and loo roll and ramen
a black bear – barely a yearling – so hot
she cannot calibrate sleep
maw open
she places paw
before paw
her bow-legged limbs all limber and lank
her cinnamon snout bearing low
in search of –
I make a list –
bird food and garbage
water and same-day salmon
here
in this counterfeit den
with its cool cool weather
she moves
that we might see her and do more
than spill our cold milk

Bottomry

perhaps the dead don't care
for the things we imagine they do
how we wronged them and mean to waste
our gift above the dirt and off the mantel

perhaps they lie sovereign
while we imagine they hover
            deadweight moored to memory
            jurymasts facing the wind
            stitched to this copper sea   like the overthrown
            chained
            in that painting with the typhoon coming

and so we say
something must grow out of grief
turn then to the trees for coffin
or comfort

we say they never leave us
imagine they take root
they   burrow away from us
that last breath a way to weigh anchor
broken lanyard ending our dogwatch

perhaps the dead do not care
to turn back as the same self
and having squared away
will not be foiled
thwarted
misunderstood

perhaps they feast
on silence at long last
as swell of joy
as rest

Carolina Gold

The success of Carolina Gold only made things worse, increasing demand for slaves from western Africa, the continent's so-called Rice Coast, who knew better than anyone else how to plant and harvest it.
—Keith Pandolfi

Come out the other side and think yourself home
all waterways and river folk

it may be that coast is coast

but you no-folk here
no boat here
nothing but what brings you here
you   hand
you   boy
you   dig
you make rice grow
glow gold in all this muck

grow transplant
tiller
water panicle
from your own sweat

you   concomitant
no
you   calibrate
         irrigate
         cultivate
make
up and down the fields while *those* reapers sleep
you sow one hundred thousand acres

of southern backwater
to tidewater empire
g r a i n b y g r a i n

the day you set free from this shore
come out the other side
and call anywhere
anywhere

home

Binocular or As Fast As

Whatever chases me
through wood or up shaggy hill
apparition or man
I jog with one eye on the trees
and one on the path behind me

Let whatever watches me
see me see
in the narrow window day drags between sleep
and sleep
that leaf-thin sliver of light

How odd that I whose bones are scrimshaw
I who have held my blood with eye
and hand and know its taste as iron should ask
oh earth   mother   mothers
why is my hand forever to the plough?

I reel my mind's visit in
move almost how I wann' …want to move
slow inside the river bend
whatever is coming   tell it
pedal or foot I move sideways

Except for that one bend
that loop where outside can't see in
how fast are you the mean-looking man said
as I swept past him on a quiet road
could've been question or quelling

I'll never know
fast as I was

That night
spoon slow
between mouth and chipped bowl
I thought
did the man mean
on a level playing field
no fox or fiend
with the brightness of bodies
for safety
their eyes my eyes
oh   I thought
I'm fast
fast or slow as I wanna be

Meditations on Fugitivity

we say we and mean
as the crow flies
is not how
we [insert: Black]
people are ~~not~~ free to move

look /we never got out of the car /not in those woods /
drove straight through /had to wait to stretch or pee /
sat in the back seat while John drove /kids' palms closed
tight as a fist behind their backs /playing rhizome or root

you say *you*
and mean to split brother
from brother to pith language when each speaks
the way you say aunt and mean so many people
i want to ask
your father's sister or your mother's?
sister how? is she older or younger?
i have many words to mark where each sister stands
on the same tree
for not every branch is open to me

say to the travelling eel what you say to me
say it to the tree
and to the seed
your oranges medicines machines nutmeg oil
say go back where you came from
make small your bleak island
shore up and keep out
every wo/man
nurse and nightingale

keep your puddles and nudge the saltwind
back where it came from
give back every last Nordmann fir
each coterie of fiery blooms
each microbial cell you now call body
this path is yours to take
i would not walk it for you
i have long been orphaned
and i am unafraid
in this final beady-eyed light
that   is not my well you poison
so measure now   how wide
the bit between daffodil and faithless sky
asphalt and veldt
fog and mist
between what the open field
and the cane field mean

to yield

Briana Weighs in on the City's Learning to Walk Campaign

Marginalised BIPOC are more likely to live in food swamps, and are therefore the disproportionate targets of sellers of unhealthy items. More than 20,000 dollar stores have popped up largely in poor communities, displacing grocery stores with ultra processed foods.
—D.G. Aaron and F.C. Stanford

I. *in which the fancy TV lady begins*
I sit here but cannot do more than ask you to explain you
the why of it all / how you come to be who you are
where you are / why your very presence makes destitute
this is the land of milk and running / honey, we all carry
the weight of our dreams / the mayor has played his part
well, he is on record as saying he has and record is science
or the reading of it anyway / truth another matter entirely
but here is our audience as is mayor Baumhouse
with his blueprints and censuses and data / numbers
are facts / the fat or thin of you / but they are ratings too
the fact is your average Joe spends five hours
and forty minutes a day watching TV / you are who
they see you are / Brianna, honey
tell your story / or let these numbers tell one for you

II. *in which Briana stares gimlet eyed at the mayor in his fine blue suit*
architect, what breath we have left
we use now to love ourselves
we are black and blue with speech
and hand, placed and replaced
but we do more than try
let that be our story   but I see
you thought we were playing
the whole time Ms More and Aunt Morel were on their feet

fetching and carrying, wiping and making,
you thought your babies
prodigy.
that they swung themselves to sleep, pushed their own strollers,
and were fed by god himself.
listen
we were walking when they came to fetch us
like we were wood   a stack of sweet reed.
we made landfall despite our sea legs shaking
and shackled we walked.
we know you ain't think we much
but you thought we took to these swamps and knelt
        'fore your god
willing and on what?
        on what.
that every time you raised our bones up 'fore dawn
we took the root's route past our allotment of joy
dug deep for something you still can't see
        cos we were playing?
you thought we did all that
that we might come to here
and be learned by a suit in blue

to walk?

What Happens Now?

The Netmenders

I call to cancel the visit. *I've heard the news*, I say, *so sorry.*
Sorry yes and kind of you, the one who calls himself Oisin says
but Padraic knew, you see.
He stops and so I have to ask, *Knew what?*

Well, Oisin says.
Well, Murdo echoes, *Paddy knew time was only one kind of fish,*
he's after another now.
I'll come another day, I say.

Sure you know yourself, Oisin says, *but job's a job.*
This is another day, Murdo chimes in, *grand as any other.*
You know where to find us.
The line dies.

I'm there a minute when
without so much as a *would-you* Murdo 'fecks' rope
across a broken float. *You have to leave the hole. To let the sea t'r'u".*
I blink. *May as well feck off if you plan to catch the sea.*

See? Oisin holds up a net,
its holes the size of a two-year-old's fist.
His skin all salt leather, breath all salt air,
Let it or it'll keep you instead.

Mesh.
        Gauge.
Gillnet.
        Ghostnet.
Flounder.
        Sole.
Whitting.

I can't write fast enough to keep up with their tongues' tip,
flicker and anchor. All tongue and no familiar word to reel me in.
Hyoid bone a float between airway and story. So I stop,

listen.
I think I hear the kittiwake's black tips move,
feel its stark white belly graze the blue above us,
its call midway between frisson and song.

Murdo raises an eyebrow, *it's not blue you know.*
I barely catch the fibre he places in my hand
though I feel my fingers slip between its nylon grids.
Not blue at all.

The kittiwake? I say dumbly.
He looks at me proper
for the first time, tilting his head a little.
That, I mean.

That's just what your eye wants to see
after the wet eats all the red. It's like this,
if you travel thataways its almost as dark as our Rosie's hair
or your skin.

You have to cut and loop the fibre, Oisin says.
His large fingers swift on the overhand
Here, then backhand the knot, even-like, like so.
Cut it off, no, yes like that, then let it be.

That's how you make a net whole,
one eye on the sun
and what's left on this sea
of threads.

Murdo smiles for the first time, *Paddy'd say,*
A hole small enough for the sea
and big enough for the light and minnow
to pass t'r'u".

You, the One Leaving

'How long will you be staying?' said the officer
Stamp held clean off the page
His brow rising and rising above his grey eyes
A meadow above the tree line
And in the great big hall
A cord was loosened before and latched
Behind our traveller
It was a room of sorts with benches
And not much else
Except for the ones who couldn't answer
'How long will you be staying?'
The way the officer wanted
Our traveller touched the officer's cuff
'Tell them to travel is to see
And I've come to see the eaves and
The seracs, the very curtains and cliffs...'
The officer cut him off with a shrug
Our man left in his would-be colonnade shouts,
'The crevasses too. While we have them'
With barely a look over his shoulder
The officer turned into an officious looking room
This with walls and a heavy wooden door
And our traveller watched as other travellers passed
Without incident and tried not to look at him
He felt keenly their non-stare
Imagined eyes rolling in their soft heads
Wanting to see the man sitting in an open cage
A barrier of ropes to hold him
Retreating bodies – silhouettes shrinking in the light
'How long will you be staying?' our traveller asked
The fellow stranger never even turned her head
Her hijab unstirring in its stillness against the bench

Next to him. 'No talking' a voice bellowed out
  As the officer came out from where he'd been
His feet cropping the distance
  Our traveller heard his voice and best he could
Battened down the hatches
  His clever eyes – twin channels – now widening
An avalanche of fear settling in his belly
  But but
No wet snow
  Or calving followed
No plates or prisms or columns
  Not one flake not *this* time
Just his own feet carrying him towards seeing
  As the officer shoved his passport – stamped! –
Back into his sweaty and brown hand.

Commons

Since hunters cannot share the same forest
this is mine.
And here, whoever their mother
Country. Church. Tongue.
Children of the same belly
split the locust's head –
let no one hunger
or let all hunger.

Did we not say
when one house burns
a neighbour will surely meet the open air
his own flaming curtains in hand.
Here we gather
blistered tongue to blistered tongue and say
no one owns the forest or its flycatchers
nor its trout lilies or lichen. No one.

Not the birds or the night or the river,
who are you?
Not even the man in Pennsylvania
who cleans raw hides and places a sign to say
trespassers will be ______,
not even that man who wants everything
to himself.
Soon too much is never enough.

Show me your tongue
and tell me – what is everything?
Even the dirt which catches every footfall
must turn its head to hear the roots whisper.
We come to the forest's beginend now, brother.

You say it either stops or starts here
it cannot do both. I turn your head to watch
the beasts descend from their hills
to eat only what they can carry.
Only man, only man devours devouring.
His heart eating everything.

We watch a buck stop in the long shadow then leap out –
out still. His twisted horns victorious in his autumn rut.
Look, I say, *what boundary shall we insist upon for the air?*
Brother, descend from your hill,
no one can say this is mine
and mean anything worth hearing.
Brother,
are you no one?

Nationhood for the Domesticated

By happenstance, I moved countries and was lonely –
          something having been taken from me – and so
I got a cat and was glad of it when all the coughing came.
          Katse's been with me since she was a kitten.

I couldn't have brought an animal into the house.
          Not live, not back home – to shed and scratch,
to rub its body against furniture and mama's gift
          of curtains. The guests' ironed trouser legs.

When I told Ama I did, she said – *That's wild,*
          a whole animal inside your house. She wondered
whether it could reach the kitchen counter. *Your plates?*
          And you, do you walk uncovered in the rain now too?

I was too afraid to say that in this place
          I even brush her small teeth,
talk to her, spend time with and on her.
          Spend money on insurance just for her.

What was left of understanding between us
          was only ever a paper boat. Now half-wet
with each crossing. Language,
          all false cognate, all false friend.

          //

I should have been an owl. Turned my head to see
what was coming. My tubular eyes looking into this glaring
future. My quiet, quiet flight eating turbulence. Notwithstanding
handstands spent pondering my animal stance, I'm here now

keeping Katse off frame during our weekly Zoom. Her presence like a nice dress or the right perfume turns me into someone else – someone my friends might've laughed at. Might've called domesticated and tried to understand.

Curiosity

Wena, Kgomo / You, Cow

Ka e tlhoka ka tlhoka boroko
—Setswana riddle

wet-nosed god
you
whose absence thieves all sleep
first currency
first ruminant
cloven-hoofed thing

goddess of joy and victory
over hunger
over thirst
great leveller of men
we see you and say
even the poorest cow can birth a fine calf

bovine, head low amidst the thimble grass
and acacia pods
you are all-wind
you come tail down
come from every where
humour swaying with each handler

whose gold is wet and white?
whose dung is shelter and dressing?
fire?
friend to plant and fungus
did your horns rising in the morning mist
not give our first measure of dawn

of colour
e khunou, e khunwana
e nala, e naana
champa, e champana
I've lost nights keeping count
chasing your coat's many colours

eight of you for each son
to bring home a daughter
what dog
what friend
show me the thing more near to me
than this wide-eyed keeper of men

you have all my noons
my nights
animal, we are yoked
and something whispers my name
while I pebble the water's quiet surface
one ear to follow your bell

hand raised above the brimming river
its lily pads aquiver, it asks
who keeps who, grazier?
between the open gate of your dawn
and the dusk at which I imagine
I kraal you in

soft-eyed friend
straight-backed coat of hide and colour
shepherd of well-sung song
you who have never changed your lowing
like stars in that high and blue field
worth less to all but the one who looks

Grace

This is how I come to the trees
To the shrub and the hartebeest
Hair knotted
No wine or cigar for Baron Cimetière
No copper or cloth for Oya
Not one rock to lay on a tombstone
Today the trees are stones
They've nothing to say to me
No head or tailwind
Still I can hear you here
Where you gave yourself to everything
Drunk with air and sun trapped
In that cackle you called laughter
I come here to see you now
Let the rest keep their white flowers
The lilies and gladioli and dirt
Their graveyard
I come here in the hot light
In the cool dark
Out out in the open
Where you told a poor boy
You loved him
How you loved the trees
Even though there were none here then
I knew then Grace that I finally was safe
Held between where the shepherd tree roots
And this
That now passes for sky
Without you

Bread for the Birds: Act One

To be read in quick succession by many voices

I:	figure with a half-empty glass of water
YOU:	figure in a yellow raincoat
HER:	pregnant woman
CHILDREN:	children
HIM:	figure in a tailored suit
THEY:	young adult figure in gumboots
WE:	all/chorus

All enter stage left and right, each walking past various exit, warning and biohazard signs. Crossing a low threshold of plastic bags, masks, stacks of newspapers, bleached coral reef and an embankment with exposed roots, all stand centre-stage, packed tightly inside an acrylic box. Water slowly rises, coming up to their knees. Children of all ages sit DR and DL, their backs turned to the audience.

I

It rose above us like a god and I remember thinking
who or what would willingly give wings to such rage
but there it was and so a benefactor must exist.
Somewhere behind this communal mirror glass
a huge, angry, beastly cloud of a thing is setting its course
and likening it to mine and yours.

YOU

I remember seeing the sky as it scrunched its face,
filling its cheeks with smoke and hurling rage at every
man's door, at life's very factory gate. Huffing and puffing
till it seized, sneezed, pouring citrus rain upon us.
Yet none of us, no not one of us, knew what to call it.

HER

And since that day it always seems as though
no matter what we do, for each birth
we must give away one more than we will receive.
For each ten dead perhaps five daughters will be born
to remind us how we should have held on to what we had
before fortune called, before tomorrow was gone.

CHILDREN

For we are but bread for the birds,
dead before our very breath is heard,
light as lead feathers lost to the wind,
we sink in a quagmire of our own making.

HIM

To look at us now – we children of the poor – plastic
progeny are but jaded shopkeepers with nothing left to sell.
Merchants charmed into a blind-folded trade against a
merciless rage. And the machines – they do not even care
whether we live or die. This war to them is nothing personal.
In this war to them we are the ones on a fool's errand,
nothing but plastic bag carrying, greenhouse tail-chasers
if we but knew it.

THEY

And in this gingerbread man existence
we think ourselves gods.
We are changing things, breaking things
to live as kings
leaving costly crumbs wherever we go.

CHILDREN

Yet we are but bread for the birds.
We are the baker and the baked,
our deeds name us the sly fox
and still we are running. Running
as fast and as far as we can
from these facts and ourselves.

I

We tell ourselves that of course we bolt, go to seed.
That our sons, our daughters, all children into chaos
are born. While the air turns their gaze putrid
with inherited greed, with the loss
of everything green, they will become the perfect
puppeteer's industrial dream, for we are none of us
the light beams we should have become. None of us
it seems example what we were meant to become.

YOU

And when our life's a vigil for sun or snow,
when the ice crackles like roots against your feet of clay
will you know then the sound of death coming?
It is not loud or crass, the earth will not crash
upon itself merely to warn you of your folly.
What of the endless anatomy of greed, its bumper crop
as fleet-footed as groundsel. Haruspex, which way will
tomorrow's wind blow? And when hot becomes the new
cold will you, will we remember then what the prophets
of old foretold? How they spoke of an ungrateful tribe
turning a king's providence into a tomb.

*Here, turn your back to the audience if you are not complicit –
else join the chorus*

WE

You and I are bread for the birds, my friend.
But if by some small chance you or you or you
are a voice feral amidst this fury of uncontainable
plastic and sudden oak death, they will ask you –
who you think you are to find your own right
when everyone else is left behind. Baptist, tell them.
Tell them your castle is made of sand and air.
That you are not a tree alone – fragile,
breakable, exposed in this roofless fort.
But that thing, that nameless thing
that started it all – it was us; it was us all along.

(BLACKOUT)

Variation on the Life of Roaches

Ecological charisma describes the anatomical, geographical and temporal properties of an organism that configure its detectability by a human subject. It relates to the human umwelt: the bubble in which we make sense of the world.

—Jamie Lorimer, 'Charisma'

Roach, since I cannot sing
I offer you a spell.
A psalm to sooth all Blattodea.

You are forgiven whatever sin we imagine
weighs heavily against all
who shun the light,

scatter and flit.
Malodorous thing, all must and oil,
to what do you belong?

Let them bring their citrus,
their bay leaves and cinnamon.
Let them cast peppermint, coffee

and bleach.
Roach, you stay brimming,
every boundary a bridge.

What grace I have I gift to you who has no lungs,
bug eyed, broad backed and small headed,
we say *heathen* and mean something beneath that,

though your wings – pleat of leather and membrane –
have scuttled the earth for two hundred
and more years. Each year a span. Indiscrete mob,

nocturnal hisser, rosewood tinted pest, pet.
Most of all, your life a talent of indiscriminate love
of dark corner, forgotten stamp and damp drain.

Whoever has conceived in space will inherit the earth.
Its wretched cupboard boxes, their poorly limbed tenants.
This that has sent men flying out of their own homes

renders us slow, impotent. Makes futile our efforts
at spotless intimacy. Gregarious flyer, burrower
that makes us retch. Your sound less scurry,

more scratch and hiss. Consider what the men in robes
and the beggar share. Slight leveller, survivor of thirst,
of heat and arctic cold.

You whose name has been blasphemed.
Six-legged harbinger from whom science
mimics mechanical legs, our future hearts –

will no one sing your song?

Even the Thorns

know why we move through the thicket the way we do
or why the girl whose father has fast hands
swoops around the old oak table   and flinches
when he enters a room

        and when they said explorer
        they meant conqueror   not friend
        shrewd white teeth showing

spectre   here we are between
what the borders mean by country
and what the nightingale and eel mean by wind and water

        who turns to us now to say
        which is lawful and which right
        be it son or father it says *if* he be just

listen   she who harrows
under that circumstance of self
partus sequitur ventrem   can reap only stones

        and she who reaps stone
        need only harvest until her enemy's hand
        be taken out of the way

at that mutilated fiefdom's door
June keeps on asking
'what kind of person could…'

        empire's history lies here
        and elsewhere   in the workhouse
        and the tabernacles of time

if it is the common wealth of place you're after
artefact   we have long arrived
but I am always already on my way somewhere else

        we   all of us   tell stories
        about ourselves to ourselves
        yet what was   was   and is not

I cannot eat my words
for curses   like chickens
bide time

        behemoth
        do what you have always done
        yet look how beautiful we are in spite   of spite

outside this small theatre of the grotesque
what we must be without it
even if joy accompanies us
in our toil

The Healer

Biography or The Good News

I've stopped telling my son fairytales told to me by other folk.
Today we take the bus through Julius Nyerere Drive. Of course
we are not actually there. My son – born after I shed myself
of country and border and borders. Always so many borders
of water and paper and wall and men to cross – was born here.
He has never seen the first country.

The good news is
I was always a distracted child. Looking out classroom windows.
Half listening to the teacher's whatnots. Chasing cowpea,
milkweed and senna. Half chatting to the wind. It's a kind of
dissonance. It is. But how it clung to me is how I'm driving now.
On a bus made of memory. So vivid – it must be vivid because
Boago's laughing at nothing and waving out our makeshift window.
Shouting words I don't remember teaching him
          Pula
          Dumelang
          Metsi
          Morogo
All he will ever need to cross back and back. And back.

I stop the bus.
Take his hand as we cross the street. The early morning already hot and
dry. *Where next mama? Where next?* he shouts as I point out the passengers
in their bright and dull clothes. Their covered and bare heads.
The women's faces smooth and not with ochre. How tall and short
and ordinary they are. Boago seems distracted by their hands. *A bricklayer,*
I say, *like papa.*
How do you know? he asks.
I don't I say *but isn't it fun to guess?*
How about her? I ask
A doctor, he says. And now he makes a list. *Cook. Painter. Fisherman.*

I'm pleased with his childish choices. With the promise
of eucalyptus and dumplings in the air I stop at the bus rank
to buy him an orange flown in from whoknowswhere. After,
I think of orange blossoms and jet fuel, of filaments and fuselage.

Today we stay away from the wet north, where rivers come
from west and east to flood the salt pans. We come to the
Central Business District instead, as dry and dam-bound
as its kraal of a city. This used to be the point I'd tell him
about self-made princes and castles. About the sleeping women
of men's dreams. I no longer burden him with anything
but his whole self. A biography fit for a boy.

Today I say to Boago –
Refuse whatever storms would have you settle for lesser loves.
You were made for too-warm nights full with the frangipani's spice
and citrus. The flamingo's flamboyant call. For days spent
watching the slow explosion of beans hunching up through lush
ground. For Nok, Songhai, Mwenemutapa. The fare is only ever
a distraction. The price has already been paid. Whoever offers you
a way to survive, refuse them. You must thrive. Little matsutake,
not since I was a child have I known a paradise without thorns.
Even here, men stuff their pockets with the degradation of others.
Let no one expel you from your own life. Call it shabby. Expect
better. You must live better.

Boago is quiet then all pirouette and splutter. *B-better* he says.
Feet kicking at a plastic bag some uncanny passenger must've
dropped. His little face solemn. Feeling moving through his body,
that first country to which he belongs. Though surely, he is too
young to understand, there is a phrase his father says every time
he walks through the front door. Boago has taken to saying it
at the oddest times –
Wha's the good news? he says.

The good news is
                    you.
Youyouyou.
You who are alive
are   alive
now.

Acknowledgements

There are many people to thank for creating both the *an/other pastoral* chapbook and Another Pastoral project. Thank you to Harriet Green, Maxwell Ayamba and Michael Malay for sharing your stories and cherished places and how you engage the natural world around you. Thank you to Heather Marks, who is very likely the reason you have even heard of this book. Thank you to Eloise Stevens for working audible wonders on both Another Pastoral and the adaptation of Another Pastoral for Grapevine. Thank you to Rosalyn McLean for bringing all the strands of this project together in a breath-taking book design. Thank you to Nii Ayikwei Parkes for expertly holding each line, copy editing this collection so every word speaks volumes. Thank you to our readers, Asmaa Jama, Tsitsi Jaji, Ralph Pite and Samantha Walton, who together formed an enriching and honest editorial force that has helped shape the poems in this collection. Thank you to Chris Abani for your generous and resonant reading of *an/other pastoral.* Thank you to Tebogo Cranwell, whose minimalist and evocative illustrations speak beautifully to the poetry in this book, providing a rich invitation for those coming to sit with the words of this collection.

A number of these poems ('Commons', 'Wena, Kgomo / You, Cow' and many others) draw heavily on the proverbial and idiomatic nature of the Setswana language. The line 'even the poorest cow can birth a fine calf' is borrowed from Alec C. Campbell's (and Alice Molefe's) work on '100 Tswana Proverbs'. 'Even the Thorns' borrows the line 'what kind of person could' from June Jordan. The epigraph for 'Brianna Weighs in on the City's Learning to Walk Campaign' is from D.G. Aaron and F.C. Stanford's paper 'Is obesity a manifestation of systemic racism? A ten-point strategy for study and intervention'.

One learns from other poets of course. But thank you, too, to
all those wonderfully generous thinkers on gender, race, class,
Blackness, mobility and much more. All your digging gave this poet
an embarrassment of riches, in theory, film, song and so on,
to think alongside.

Many thanks to the curators of Lyrikline for publishing 'Bread for
the Birds' (an early version of 'Bread for the Birds: Act One').

Thank you to Arts Council England, for giving me the space
to write.

Thank you to Lily Green and No Bindings for your vision and
unwavering support – for holding together the many threads of
an/other pastoral with such care and patience. This has been an
extraordinary partnership.

And thank you to Kirk B. Sides for always being there and always
knowing what to say.

About Another Pastoral

This book forms part of the wider Another Pastoral project, a collaboration between poet Tjawangwa Dema and No Bindings' director, Lily Green. Through the project, Lily and Tjawangwa created an audio piece and archive with three people whose work and interests centre on how we experience nature, especially as People of Colour in the UK: Maxwell Ayamba, Michael Malay and Lily's mother, Harriet Green.

Follow these instructions to listen to *Another Pastoral* and explore the Another Pastoral Archive:

Using WhatsApp, simply send a photo of any of the illustrations in this book to (+44) 7380333721, then follow the directions in the WhatsApp chat.

Another Pastoral

an/other pastoral by Tjawangwa Dema
with illustrations by Tebogo Cranwell
and a foreword by Chris Abani
Published by No Bindings, 2022
Readers Dr Samantha Walton, Dr Tsitsi Jaji, Asmaa Jama
Copy Editor Nii Ayikwei Parkes
Proofreader Alexandra Holmes
Designer Rosalyn McLean

Another Pastoral by Lily Green
with Tjawangwa Dema
First broadcast on BBC Radio 6 Music on BBC Introducing Arts
with Gemma Cairney on 7th December 2020
Interviewees Maxwell Ayamba, Michael Malay, Harriet Green
Editing and Sound Design Eloise Stevens
Producer Edson Burton
Executive Producer Steve Gear
A Calling the Shots production for New Creatives.
New Creatives is supported by Arts Council England and BBC Arts.

Another Pastoral Archive
Made available by No Bindings and Grapevine
Archivists Maxwell Ayamba, Michael Malay, Harriet Green
Grapevine Tim Kindberg, Lily Green

Another Pastoral is supported using public funding by the National Lottery through Arts Council England